The Little Black Book: Of Inspiration

by Rebekah S. Harper

DORRANCE PUBLISHING CO
EST. 1920
PITTSBURGH, PENNSYLVANIA 15238

Dorrance Publishing Co
585 Alpha Drive
Suite 103
Pittsburgh, PA 15238
Visit our website at *www.dorrancebookstore.com*

ISBN: 979-8-8860-4136-1
eISBN: 979-8-8860-4801-8

Contents of this book

Chapter 1. DOs and DON'Ts 1

Chapter 2. I AM NOW.... 3

Chapter 3. BE.... 5

Chapter 4. I NOW RELEASE.... I NOW GIVE.... 7

Chapter 5. SPECIAL MESSAGES 9

Chapter 6. SPECIAL AFFIRMATION 11

THIS BOOK IS DEDICATED TO MY FAMILY

WORDS OF WISDOM:
I now forgive myself of past mistakes and
give myself permission to move forward.

Preface

This book is for the individual who seeks true change to occur in their life, and the lives around them. A person who wants to see a bright future for themselves. This book is intended to spark new ideas and thoughts to bring about positive change.

Note to reader from author:
Thank you so very much for picking this wonderful book!
I know the contents of this book
were written just for you, dear reader.
Sincerely, Rebekah S. Harper

Chapter 1

DOs and DON'Ts

1. Do act in kindness

2. Do to others as you would like them to do to you

3. Do work without grief

4. Do listen without anger

5. Do what is correct the first time

6. Do your own self-healing ritual

7. Do respect others

8. Do respect your parents and guardians

9. Do with pure intentions

10. Do believe that good prevails

11. Don't try to change people

12. Don't try to control people

13. Don't use others to fulfill yourself

14. Don't project your emotions on to others

15. Don't allow others to project their emotions on to you

16. Don't allow people to use you

17. Don't allow your insecurity to stop you from moving forward

18. Don't project your failures on to someone else's dreams

19. Don't waste your own time

20. Don't prejudge anyone

Chapter 2

I AM NOW…

1. I am now so very happy

2. I am now calm and relaxed

3. I am now at my best

4. I am now loving to those around me

5. I am now patient

6. I am now so very strong

7. I am now brave

8. I am now filled with love

9. I am now free of all things that limit me

10. I am now optimistic

11. I am now myself at all times

12. I am now honest with myself and divine

13. I am now working in alignment with my purpose

14. I am now whole and healthy

15. I am now at peace with myself

16. I am now in control of my emotions

17. I am now self-motivating

18. I am now proud to be myself

19. I am now happy doing what I love

20. I am now encouraged to be myself

Chapter 3

BE…

1. Be you at your best

2. Be the change you want to see

3. Be kind to yourself

4. Be honest with yourself

5. Be happy to be you

6. Be the creator you were born to be

7. Be wise in all situations

8. Be good to yourself

9. Be good to others

10. Be patient at all times

11. Be not afraid of the future

12. Be patient with others

13. Be in control of your emotions

14. Be aware of your actions

15. Be careful of how you speak to people (no matter the age)

16. Be careful of what you think

17. Be careful of what you speak over yourself

18. Be careful of what you speak over others

19. Be not conformed to this world

20. Be the one who brings true changes into your family's lives

Chapter 4

I NOW RELEASE… I NOW GIVE…

1. I now release fear

2. I now release anger

3. I now release all past events that don't bring about positive change

4. I now release all bad habits

5. I now release people, places, and things that no longer serve me

6. I now release negative energy

7. I now release negative thoughts of myself

8. I now release envy

9. I now release jealousy

10. I now release greed

11. I now give myself permission to release all things that don't belong to me

12. I now give myself permission to love myself completely

13. I now give myself permission to trust myself

14. I now give with an open heart to those who deserve it

15. I now give up old habits that limit my growth

16. I now give up the need to be right

17. I now give up the desire to control

18. I now give up my unwillingness to focus on myself

19. I now give up all thoughts that hold me in the past

20. I now give up my ego and old thoughts of myself that no
longer serve me and my highest good

Chapter 5

SPECIAL MESSAGES

MESSAGE 1 FOR THE AWKWARD

Hi reader! It is I, Rebekah S. Harper. I just wanted to tell you that, it's never wrong to be who you are. Love the skin you are in! No one can take what has always been yours.

MESSAGE 2 FOR THE FEARFUL

Hello reader! I, Rebekah S. Harper, must tell you that you were never born with the energy or belief of fear. It is a construct to put you in a negative frequency that doesn't belong to you. May positive energy abound, dear reader.

MESSAGE 3 FOR THE UNBELIEVER

Hi, darling! It is I, Rebekah S. Harper. I want you to know that the proof you seek is within you. Dear reader, the light you seek is the light that shines in your eyes. You are the proof of all things possible if you so believe it. You must find yourself, dear reader. That will make all the difference.

MESSAGE 4 FOR THE ANGRY

Hi, honey! It's me, Rebekah S. Harper. I know what has happened to you wasn't fair or right; I can only offer understanding, dear reader. You must allow the truth to be what it is. What has happened, if it's now or in the past, you must know God/Karma is always working. Let go! Allow these things to work for you.

Side note FOR THE ANGRY

Dear reader, I had to reread this message for myself several times to better grasp this powerful message. The freedom of letting go will allow your true destiny to unfold, may positive energy abound.

Sincerely, RSH

Chapter 6

SPECIAL AFFIRMATIONS

1. I am kind

2. I am optimistic

3. I am encouraging

4. I am confident

5. I am honest

6. I am strong

7. I am brave

8. I am secure

9. I am good

10. I am free

11. I am aware

12. I am calm

13. I am relaxed

14. I am action

15. I am positive

16. I am abundance

17. I am whole

18. I am complete

19. I am worthy of love

20. I am worthy of honesty

21. I am worthy of a life I want

22. I am a creator

23. I am more than who I was before

24. I am never without

25. I am good enough

26. I am not in control of others

27. I am only in control of myself

28. I am my thoughts

29. I am sure of myself

30. I am peace

31. I am divine

32. I am now at my very best

Just a few lovely affirmations, dear reader!
If you like, you could add some of your own. Be my guest!

Next page for BONUS READ
"TO MY LOVER" BY AN'OMAGE

A POEM "TO MY LOVER"

Dear lover, you have allowed me to shine from the outside in! Dear one who holds me close all the days of this life! I will see you again. Over and over again, I will seek you out and find you! Oh God, I so adore you and trust that you will forever love this creator you have created! My dearest love, Yahweh. I will hold you close.

ABOUT THE AUTHOR

Rebekah S. Harper was born in Columbia, South Carolina and graduated from Ridge View High. She currently has four wonderful channels on YouTube, Facebook, Instagram, and Likee called MRS SEED OF THE DAY where she gives only life experience advice in hopes of encouraging people of all walks of life to be the best vision of themselves. If you would like to follow or subscribe the following is the correct spelling for each site enjoy!

YOUTUBE: mrsseedoftheday
FACEBOOK: mrsseedoftheday
INSTAGRAM: mrsseedoftheday
LIKEE: mrsseedoftheday
TikTok: mrsseedoftheday